Dear Readers,

   I started a dayhome 7 years ago to raise my sons. Learning became a high priority, which meshes well with my desire to include children learning where food comes from and all the discoveries nature has to offer.

   I continue to learn about gardening for my own children, and the children whom I help raise.

   This book is for you, Teeias and Shiloh ... may you always explore where your food comes from and the benefits of nature and learning.

Jennie

Jennie is a Child and Youth Care Counsellor based in Alberta, Canada. Having worked in the social services field for 15 years, she took a hiatus to raise her two boys at home, while also creating and running an established day home.

This new adventure allowed her to see the world through much smaller eyes than the teenagers she typically worked with. This new insight propelled her passion for photography and telling the stories of her boys' Blackfoot culture.

Jennie is also a gardening, photography, quilting & sewing hobbyist.

JENNIE EAGLESPEAKER

Please don't hide my vegetables

There's so much that I can learn

Picking out
a rainbow

From each and
every spot

MORE FROM EAGLESPEAKER PUBLISHING

AUTHENTICALLY INDIGENOUS GRAPHIC NOVELS:
UNeducation: A Residential School Graphic Novel
Napi the Trixster: A Blackfoot Graphic Novel
UNeducation, Vol 2

AUTHENTICALLY INDIGENOUS COLORING BOOKS:
Napi: A Coloring Experience
UNeducation: A Coloring Experience
Completely Capricious Coloring Collection
A Day at the Powwow (grayscale coloring)

AUTHENTICALLY INDIGENOUS KIDS BOOKS:
Teeias Goes To A Powwow

AUTHENTICALLY INDIGENOUS NAPI CHILDREN'S BOOKS:
Napi and the Rock
Napi and the Bullberries
Napi and the Wolves
Napi and the Buffalo
Napi and the Chickadees
Napi and the Coyote
Napi and the Elk
Napi and the Gophers
Napi and the Mice
Napi and the Prairie Chickens
Napi and the Bobcat
... and many more to come

www.eaglespeaker.com

If you absolutely loved this book (or even just kind of liked it), please find it on amazon.com and leave a quick review. Your words help more than you may realize

Made in the USA
Middletown, DE
12 August 2024

58947514R00020